Understanding

a few concepts in

Islam

By

P. M. Mohsin

ISBN: 1-4107-0778-4 (e-book)
ISBN: 1-4107-0779-2 (Paperback)

This book is printed on acid free paper.

1stBooks - rev. 03/26/04

In the name of the Merciful,
Who has provided guidance
for all,
who seek,
O Allah!
You are apparent through Your
creations,
a continuous Manifestation,
a natural Glorification!
Those who read
and those who learn
and set out in
Your search
find You Omnipresent,
as
You are apparent through Your
creations,
a continuous Manifestation,
a natural Glorification.

Contents

Introductory remarks vii
The belief of One God in Islam 1
The concept of Justice in Islam 11
Focusing The Human Justice 14
The Prophet and the Book 17
The concept of Intelligence in Islam 23
The concept of Prayers in Islam 24
Fasting during the month of Ramadan 28
The concept of Alms giving in Islam 30
Hajj *(The pilgrimage to the House of God in Mecca)* 31
The concept of Jihad in Islam 34
Male or Female 41
The Resurrection and the Hereafter 43
Jesus son of Mary (peace be upon them) 47
A few objective views on Islam 50
The Food 52
Some of the words of prophet Muhammad (S) 53
About the Author 94

Note: There are only a limited number of Qur'anic verses quoted in this book, but Qur'an cites quite a few verses on the topics covered in this publication.

Introductory remarks

What do we mean, when we say Islam? Who are the Muslims?

Islam is a way that over 1.3 billion people in the world* have adopted, to reach a particular destiny: *the peace here and a peaceful hereafter.*

The term *Islam* has the word *S-L-M* at its roots, signifying *peace and submission.* Thus a Muslim attains peace and serenity physically, psychologically, and spiritually by submitting to the will of God instead of one's own impulse and worldly compulsions. It is this concept of submission only to the God that frees one from internal and external conflicts and chaos. Islam means submission to the will of One God - *the God referred in Arabic as Allah, the word originated by Arabic words – Al* (the) *& Ilah* (God), thus Allah *The God.* The peace that is supposed to flow from this submission, establishes a calm in one's self and one's surroundings.

The word *Muslim* means *the one who submits* to the will of Allah.

A Muslim submits to Allah, as the Creator and Sustainer of the universe, the God of Mercy, who sent the prophets such as Noah, Abraham, Moses, and Jesus (p.b.u.t.^) earlier and prophet Muhammad (S) as the last messenger. By acknowledging and professing the *Oneness of God and the prophet-hood of prophet Muhammad (S)* without any compulsion, one basically becomes a Muslim. Being faithful, however, depends on the way one follows the last messenger of peace, and commits oneself for gradual improvements physically, intellectually, spiritually and socially.

A Muslim is supposed to fulfill the purpose of his/her creation as a human being by following Islam.

Islam is a comprehensive system that leads Muslims to a completely fulfilled life as human beings, and thus leads them to attain a peaceful destiny. For example, as Islam is concerned with individual as well as collective well being of human societies, therefore, among other things, learning and seeking knowledge is especially emphasized in Islam, because it increases individual and collective awareness, comprehension, and faith. As a process of spiritual advancement, and to stay healthy physically, and mentally, a Muslim abides by some sophisticated dietary, hygienic, and precautionary practices, as well as some moral principles, individually and socially.

It is quite amazing, however, that in spite of ample information available on the true essence of Islam, how media not only avoids mentioning constructive contributions of Muslims, but often chooses certain individuals to present its opinion about Islam and Muslims in such a contradictory manner that is not only alien, but demeaning to Islam and Muslims. This fulfills no other purpose except to further misinform, and mislead the audiences, and to introduce a misunderstanding that already exists, in a highly dramatic way. By widening the gap among the people of world they may actually be doing a disservice to the efforts of a collective human progress of modern societies. It is not a hidden fact that the modern advances in science and technology were to a large degree a contribution of Muslim scholars and scientists.

It would be an unfortunate state of affair, where the scholastic energies of Muslim minds go unutilized in part due to the propagated biases. It would be helpful on the other hand if the open-minded people in the media invite Muslim scholars to establish a constructive dialogue for the sake of positive human progress, and peace. They could join hands with those scholars, who benefit from their search of Islamic sciences and literature, as it continues to astonish and guide contemporary intellectuals, and the researchers of modern times:

'It ... seemed impossible to explain how a text produced at the time of the Qur'an could have contained facts that have only been discovered in modern times...' (Dr. Maurice Bucaille)

The following pages are thus intended to provide a helpful and *brief* account of a few concepts in Islam. Readers may find the following pages oriented towards exploring a dimension of 'whys', rather than 'hows' about some of the beliefs and practices in Islam.

^ Peace be upon them

*By the beginning of 21st century.

Further more there are more Muslims in the United States of America than some of the Middle Eastern countries, such as Bahrain, Jordan, Kuwait, Oman, and United Arab Emirates. Actually there are more Muslims living in the US than there are in Bahrain, Kuwait, Qatar, and United Arab Emirates combined.

One God

In the name of Allah, the Beneficent,
the Merciful.

"And your Lord is the Self-sufficient One, the Lord of Mercy…" (Qur'an 6:133)

The oneness of God carries a unique meaning in Islam, oneness not in terms of numbers but in a sense that there is no one like Him. The power of human reasoning is unable to comprehend Him, and human vision is blurred when it tries to focus beyond the boundaries of physical horizon, because anything beyond the limits of time and space is beyond human comprehension, as everything inside the boundaries of time and space is limited. Limited in a sense that it occupies a space and exists in certain time; and anything that exists inside the womb of time and space is dependent on something else for its existence and sustenance, and everything that is dependent on something else could never be God.

"Allah – there is no god but He; His are the very best names" (Qur'an 20:8)

According to Islam the uniqueness of one God can never be fully comprehended, but He manifests Himself as:

AR-RAHMAN (The Beneficent)
AR-RAHIM (The Merciful)
AL-MALIK (The Sovereign Lord)
AL-QUDDUS (The Holy)
AS-SALAM (The Source of Peace)
AL-MU'MIN (The Guardian of Faith)
AL-MUHAYMIN (The Protector)
AL-'AZIZ (The Mighty)
AL-JABBAR (The Compeller)
AL-MUTAKABBIR (The Majestic)
AL-KHALIQ (The Creator)
AL-BARI' (The Evolver)
AL-MUSAWWIR (The Fashioner)
AL-GHAFFAR (The Forgiver)
AL-QAHHAR (The Subduer)
AL-WAHAAB (The Bestower)

AR-RAZZAQ (The Provider)

AL-FATTAH (The Opener)

AL-'ALIM (The All-Knowing)

AL-QABID (The Constrictor)

AL-BASIT (The Expander)

AL-KHAFID (The Abaser)

AR-RAFI' (The Exalter)

AL-MU'IZZ (The Honorer)

AL-MUZILL (The Dishonorer)

AS-SAMI' (The All-Hearing)

AL-BASIR (The All-Seeing)

AL-HAKAM (The Judge)

AL-'ADL (The Just)

AL-LATIF (The Subtle One)

AL-KHABIR (The Aware)

AL-HALIM (The Forbearing One)

AL-'AZIM (The Great One)

AL-GHAFUR (The All-Forgiving)

ASH-SHAKUR (The Appreciative)

AL-ALIYY (The Most High)

AL-KABIR (The Most Great)

AL-HAFIZ (The Preserver)

AL-MUQIT (The Maintainer)

AL-HASIB (The Reckoner)

AL-JALIL (The Sublime One)

AL-KARIM (The Generous One)

AR-RAQIB (The Watchful)

AL-MUJIB (The Responsive)

AL-WASI' (The All-Embracing)

AL-HAKIM (The Wise)

AL-WADUD (The Loving)

AL-MAJID (The Most Glorious One)

AL-BAITH (The Resurrector)

ASH-SHAHID (The Witness)

AL-HAQQ (The Truth)

AL-WAKIL (The Trustee)

AL-QAWI (The Most Strong)

AL-MATIN (The Firm One)

AL-WALI (The Protecting Friend)

AL-HAMID (The Praiseworthy)

AL-MUHSI (The Reckoner)

AL-MUBDI (The Originator)

AL-MU'ID (The Restorer)

AL-MUHYI (The Giver of Life)

AL-MUMIT (The Creator of Death)

AL-HAYY (The Alive)

AL-QAYYUM (The Self-Subsisting)

AL-WAJID (The Finder)

AL-MAJID (The Noble)

AL-WAHID (The Unique)

AL-AHAD (The One)

AS-SAMAD (The Eternal)

AL-QADIR (The Able)

AL-MUQTADIR (The Powerful)

AL-MUQADDIM (The Expediter)

AL-MU'AKHKHIR (The Delayer)

AL-AWWAL (The First)

AL-AKHIR (The Last)

AZ-ZAHIR (The Manifest)

AL-BATIN (The Hidden)

AL-WALI (The Governor)

AL-MUTA'ALI (The Most Exalted)

AL-BARR (The Source of All Goodness)

AT-TAWWAB (The Acceptor of Repentance)

AL-MUNTAQIM (The Avenger)

AL-'AFUW (The Pardoner)

AR-RA'UF (The Compassionate)

MALIK-UL-MULK (The Eternal Owner of Sovereignty)

DHUL-JALAL-WAL-IKRAM (The Lord of Majesty and Bounty)

AL-MUQSIT (The Equitable)

AL-JAME' (The Gatherer)

AL-GHANI (The Self-Sufficient)

AL-MUGHNI (The Enricher)

AL-MANI (The Preventer)

AD-DARR (The Distresser)

AN-NAFI' (The Propitious)

AN-NUR (The Light)

AL-HADI (The Guide)

AL-BADI (The Incomparable)

AL-BAQI (The Everlasting)

AL-WARITH (The Supreme Inheritor)

AR-RASHID (The Guide to the Right Path)

AS-SABUR (The Patient)

Most of the people can comprehend the depth of these attributes and names only to a certain degree.

Only the Prophets and those with higher level of knowledge and comprehension can grasp the actual realities of these names.

Prophet Muhammad's (S)[°] one of the most trusted and truthful supporters Ali (k.v.) was asked "O Commander of the Faithful! Hast thou seen thy Lord?" Ali (k.v.) immediately replied from the pulpit of the mosque in Kufa "... I would not be worshipping a lord whom I have not seen." He was asked again "O Commander of the Faithful! How didst Thou see Him?" 'Ali (k.v.) answered, "...Eyes see him not through sight's observation, but hearts see Him through the verities of faith... Verily, my Lord is subtle in subtlety, but He is not described by subtleness; tremendous in tremendousness but not described by tremendousness; grand in grandeur, but not described by grandness; and majestic in majesty, but not described by greatness. Before all things He was; it is not said that anything was before Him. After

---

° (S) and (k.v.) are the first letters of respectful phrases stated in Islamic tradition after the names of Prophet Muhammad and Ali-ibn-Abitaleb respectively.

all things He will be; it is not said that He possesses an 'after'. He willed (all) thing, not through resolution. He is all-perceiving, not through any artifice. He is in all things, but not mixed with them, nor separate from them. He is Outward, not according to the explanation of being immediate (to the senses); Manifest, not through the appearance of a vision (of Him); Separate, not through distance; Near not through approach; Subtle, not through corporealization; Existent, not after nonexistence; Active not through coercion; Determining, not through movement; Desiring, not through resolution; Hearing, not through means; and Seeing, not through organs.

Spaces encompass Him not, times accompany Him not, attributes delimit Him not and slumbers seize Him not.

By His giving sense to sense organs it is known that He has no sense organs. By His giving substance to substances it is known that He has no substances. By His causing opposition among things it is known that He has no opposite. By His causing affiliation among affairs it is known that He has no affiliate. He opposed darkness to light, obscurity to clarity, moisture to solidity, and heat to cold. He joins together those things, which are hostile to one another, and separates those things, which are near. They prove (the existence of) their Separator by their separation and their Joiner by their junction. This is (the meaning of) His words – He is the Mighty and Majestic – *And of everything created We two kinds; haply you will remember (Qur'an: LI, 49)*. So through them He separated 'before' and 'after' that it might be known that He has no before and after. They testify with their temperaments that He who gave them temperaments has no temperament. They announce through their subjection to time that He who has subjected them to time is not subject to it Himself.

He veiled some of them from others so that it might be known that there is no veil between Him and His creations other than His creation. He was a Lord when there was none over whom He was Lord; a God when there none for whom to be a God; a Knower when there was nothing to be known; and Hearer when there was nothing to be heard…He was, when there was no light by which to seek illumination, and no darkness bent over the horizons.

So our Lord is counter to creatures, all of them, and to all that is described in imaginations…'[*]

Such answers have illuminated the path that led to the submission to the will of God.

> "…Is there doubt about Allah, the Maker of the heavens and the earth…" (Qur'an 14:10)

---

[*] Translation by William, C.C.

The Justice

The purpose of every creation is inherent in its nature given to it by its Creator, as it follows a particular path assigned to it by its Creator. It is the Divine justice that has given everything its unique place in the chain of causes and affects, and sustained the universe for billions of years. From the subatomic particles to the horizons of galaxies, things have been continuously created, *transformed*, and sustained from the beginning of the time. A *dynamic* balance and a logical destiny for everything, inherent in its nature and natural course, reflect Divine wisdom and justice, and manifest the Ultimate Reality; manifest the oneness of Allah. The Unity is reflected in the interwoven diversity.

"And the heavens, He raised it high, and He made the balance,…" (Qur'an 55:7)

"And the sun runs on to a term appointed for it; that is the ordinance of the Mighty, the Knowing. And (as for) thc moon, We have ordained for it stages till it becomes again as an old dry palm branch. Neither is it allowable to the sun that it should overtake the moon, nor can the night outstrip the day; and all float on in a sphere." (Qur'an 36:38 – 40)

"...My mercy encompasses all things..."

(Qur'an 7:156)

Human beings by virtue of their created nature were also given a unique place. They were created higher beings, with the possibilities of ascending beyond angels as a virtuous being, or falling below the animal level as a materialistic being. They would reflect by choice. Unlike other creations, which are predestined to follow a particular course, such as trees or honeybees, the actions of human beings are the outcomes of their thoughts and determinations. Their conduct would reflect the degree of freedom, as they were made responsible for doing justice by keeping the balance. A much higher level of awareness, and their inclination towards doing good, and doing justice manifest that they are spiritual beings. They are neither totally independent nor fully predestined. By the capacity of knowledge that would make them dominate their habitat, they would determine their destiny; they were given the trust. They are responsible for doing justice in every aspect of life, individually, socially, and globally.

> "We have sent Our messengers with clear proofs, and We have sent down with them, the Book and the Balance, so that people may establish themselves with justice..."
>
> (Qur'an 57:25)

Focusing The Human Justice

Justice - ***In the language of law:***

Perform the duties and abstain from the prohibited factors

"…We do not impose on any soul a duty except to the extent of its ability;…" (Qur'an 6:152)

Justice - ***In the language of rights:***

To give everyone his/her rights or what they deserve (or to give everything its actual place)

"And keep up the balance with equity…." (Qur'an 55:9)

Justice - ***In the language of morality:***

To adopt every goodness and abstain from every negativity

"...he who has done an atom's weight of good shall see it.
And he who has done an atom's weight of evil shall see it."
(Qur'an 99:7-8)

Among other fascinating aspects, the capacity for acquiring faith and universal knowledge marks distinct human features, as well as demand moral responsibility on part of human beings. Human beings as a multidimensional, and multicultural being are inherently different from other social animals. Various theories were, however, put forward regarding the origins of life, but they were limited in scope, focusing the materialistic aspect of human beings from a sociological point of view. Other factors, such as psychological and spiritual aspects were ignored. It deviated a good number of people, for one reason or another, from realizing their spiritual destiny. But as human beings focus the skies in search of their origin, they are really, undermining such theories.

"Whatever benefit comes to you (O human being), it is from Allah, and whatever misfortune befalls you, it is from yourself…" (Qur'an 4:79)

"And your Lord does not deal unjustly with any one" (Qur'an 18:49)

"…And if you count Allah's favors, you will not be able to number them…"

(Qur'an 14:34)

The Prophet and the Book

This world is the part of a sophisticated and powerful system, where a magnificent balance is kept for billions of years through a remarkable and forceful guiding system. In this dynamic system different forces are at work at various layers, following a particular set of rules for a specific sub-system. The dynamic sophistication in every thing, manifested in its nature is the result of divine intention. The divine guidance actually guides everything to its goal; the degree of guidance varies with the natural capacities of the receiver.

In their own particular systems, for instance, honeybees receive guidance; so do human beings, but the modes, nature, and the power of the messages differ tremendously according to the characteristics of a being, and the tasks expected of that creature. Human beings due to their created nature are vested with various powers, such as physical, intellectual, psychological and spiritual that require a particular way of guidance. They need to know the actual rules they can apply to utilize these powers properly to achieve the optimum balance in their lives, and the proper ways to sustain it.

Prophets and Messengers with their higher individual capacities, faith and conviction had been chosen to deliver the guidance they receive in forms of revelations, and guide human beings towards a secure destiny. The true prophets teach human beings ways and wisdoms to acquire and sustain true equilibrium needed for the human prosperity. It includes the ways and wisdoms of promoting good and preventing evil to bring about peace individually and socially.

"(All) people are a single community; so Allah raised prophets as bearers of good news and as warners…" (Qur'an 2:213)

"And We did not send before you any but men to whom We sent revelation – so ask the followers of the Reminder if you do not know." (Qur'an 16:43)

"The Knower of the unseen! So He does not reveal His secrets to any, except to him whom He chooses as an apostle;" (Qur'an 72:26-27)

Prophet Muhammad (S) was chosen as the last Messenger (*Rasool*), the seal of the prophets to show people the path that leads to peaceful destiny. The prominent prophets who were chosen for guidance before him include prophets Adam, Noah, Abraham, Moses, and Jesus (Peace be upon them).

Prophet Muhammad (S), the descendant of prophet Abraham through his son prophet Ishmael (p.b.u.t) was known as Truthful and Trustworthy before receiving the Revelation, and was the embodiment of blessings, justice and morality. The light of prophecy emanated from him, as he had a very attractive personality, suited only to the prophet of his caliber; the rays of serenity, and the brightness of knowledge and wisdom radiated from him, illuminating the path of his followers to this day. People at the time observed signs of a prophet in him, including the birthmark by his shoulders; Christian monks and those who were expecting the prophet, prophesized in their book by earlier prophets, witnessed these signs. People who came into contact with him were transformed. He was sent as a blessing, and the miracle he received as a revealed book continues to guide the humanity. Qur'an, the revealed book manifests the Islamic principles, and prophet Muhammad (S) is the manifestation of Qur'an.

The Qur'an, the revealed book to prophet Muhammad (S), is unique as an everlasting miracle for the last fourteen centuries.

"A revelation from He who created the earth and highest heavens"
(Qur'an 20:4)

"...Guiding to the truth and to the right path"
(Qur'an 46:30)

"...There is none who can change His words..."
(Qur'an 6:115)

"... and most surely it is a Mighty book:
Falsehood shall not come to it from before it nor from behind it; a revelation from the Wise, the Praised One." (Qur'an 41:41-42)

Its original words and verses have guided human beings in every continent, and the book has been carried in the hands and hearts of people throughout the globe. Devotion of its followers has been reflected in multicultural settings. People in every profession continue to witness its miraculous guidance, as its verses encourage acquiring knowledge and scientific facts. The Qur'anic verses encourage reading, intellectual endeavor, and discourse.

"Most surely in the creation of the heavens and the earth and the alteration of the night and the day, and the ships that run in the sea with that which profits human beings, and the water that Allah sends down from the cloud, then gives life with it to the earth after its death and spreads in it all (kinds of) animals, and the changing of the winds and the cloud made subservient between the heavens and the earth, there are signs for a people who understand." (Qur'an 2:164)

As Muslim scholars explored the nature of creations, they discovered profound justice and wisdom behind every creation, which pointed the way to their Creator. As a result, they led the way, especially in the eighth and ninth centuries, and produced magnificent works in subjects such as astronomy, physics, mathematics, chemistry, medicine, law, ethics, philosophy, arts, architecture and literature. They laid the foundations of modern advances in human knowledge, especially in the fields of science and technology. *

---

* 100 Muslim Scientists, published in 2000, Mumbai, India.

Being Intelligent is considered to be at least a threefold concept in Islam:

(a) to know the truth and reality of the matter

"Are those who know and those who do not know alike?." (Qur'an 39:9)

(b) to distinguish between right and wrong

"You are the best of the nations raised up for (the benefit of) human beings; you enjoin what is right and forbid the wrong and believe in Allah;..." (Qur'an 3:110)

(c) to promote good and prevent evil

"Surely Allah enjoins doing of justice and the doing of good (to others) and the giving to the kindred, and He forbids indecency and evil and rebellion; He admonishes you that you may be mindful" (Qur'an 16:90)

Prayers

One of the main purposes of Islamic prayers is taken as human journey towards the Merciful. A spiritual and intellectual ascension, physical well-being, and elevation from degrading desires and its consequences. Remembrance of Allah is not supposed to be for the sole intention of only worldly benefit, or fear, although, as a result, one inevitably gains benefits in many different forms. One of the major aspirations of submission is to seek His nearness - a human effort - although, according to Islamic teachings, He is closer to us than our jugular vein.

When Muslims pray they submit, and reflect His oneness as human beings. Prayers are performed with the recognition that He does not need our prayers or praise, but deserves it; we are the ones, who need His Mercy and Help. Some prayers are performed individually, and some with congregation, but the link between a human being, and the Sustainer is always direct. From sincere submissions emanates the actual peace that embraces one's self and surroundings. As harmony flourish, the person consequently gains physical and psychological calm, as well as spiritual, moral, and ethical elevation. Social peace and justice is the natural outcome, if prayers are performed properly.

Cleanliness is considered half of the faith by Muslims, and an essential prerequisite for prayers. Muslims are required to pray (perform salat) five times a day (in every 24 hours), although it does not take more than five to ten minutes each time, but it keeps them fresh and punctual all day. Congregational prayers are encouraged, but some prayers such as Friday noon prayers are offered in congregation at a mosque, as it enhances social coherence, and eliminates racial and class differences. Friday is considered to be a holiday by Muslims. When they pray they face towards *Ka'bah*, a sanctity and the House of God, built in Mecca, by prophet Abraham and his son prophet Ishmael (p.b.u.t.). These prayers are supposed to keep Muslims away from all that is negative, and furnish inner strengths.

"And (as for) the believing men and the believing women, they are guardians of each other; they enjoin good and forbid evil and keep up prayer and pay the poor-rate, and obey Allah and His Apostle (as for) these, Allah will show mercy to them; surely Allah is Mighty, Wise." (Qur'an 9:71)

"Those who keep up prayers and pay poor-rate and they are certain of the hereafter."

(Qur'an 31:4)

"Surely the prayer keeps (one) away from indecency and evil…"

(Qur'an 29:45)

Daily required prayers, fasting during the month of Ramadan, paying alms, performing Hajj**, promoting good, and forbidding evil are a few different ways a Muslim attains nearness to God.

The meaning of prayer is unique in Islam; Muslims can literally spend every moment of their life in the state of submission to God. For example, working hard and honestly to acquire knowledge, good livelihood,

---

** Hajj will be explained later.

and to work for the benefit of the humanity, etc., are considered various aspects of submission to God.

Fasting

"O you who believe! fasting is prescribed for you, as it was prescribed for those before you, so that you may guard (against evil)"

(Qur'an 2:183)

Fasting brings about amazing reforms in those who fast. The month of fasting may arrive in hot summer days or cool winter months, but Muslims fast during the sunlight for a whole month, (*during Ramadan – the ninth month of Islamic calendar*) 29-30 days every year. It not only carries one closer to the Creator, but also transforms one physically, psychologically, and spiritually. Improved discipline, will power, and compassion are some of the outcomes. It also brings about social improvements as thirst and hunger experienced during the days of fasting allow Muslims to feel for the deprived and impoverished around the globe. Restraining oneself strictly from any misconduct intentional or unintentional during the whole month is supposed to bring about positive change significantly. Consequently piety is achieved. People, who are sick or traveling do not fast, but they can either make up the fast for the days they missed or feed the poor and hungry instead. Muslims around the world celebrate the first day after the end of Ramadan as Eid-day by thanking Allah, offering prayers, giving alms, and visiting each others houses, etc. Thus fasting during the month of Ramadan, like many other Islamic practices, carries individual as well as social benefits.

Alms (Zakat)

"…and give wealth out of love for Him to the near of kin and the orphans and the poor and the wayfarer and needy and for those in the bondage, and keep up the prayers and pay the poor-rate…" (Qur'an 2:177)

Helping out those in need in such a way that they can get back to a respectful life is highly encouraged in Islam. Showing mercy to Allah's creations is considered a noble deed and one gets back whatever one gives manifold. Zakat is actually quite a small portion that an able Muslim gives to the people in need. Besides the requirements, it is also encouraged to make contributions to the extent of one's ability. Muslims are, however, taught to be on the giving side rather than on the receiving end.

Hajj (A pilgrimage to Mecca)

Nearly two million Muslims around the world ***from different cultural and ethnic backgrounds*** travel every year to go to the city of Mecca. Muslims are required to go for pilgrimage to the House of God, in the city of Mecca, once in their life, only if they don't have any physical or financial constraints.

They go to the House of God built by the prophet Abraham and his son prophet Ishmael (p.b.u.t.). They perform prayers, and fulfill various requirements.

"And when We fixed for Abraham the place of the House, saying: Do not associate with Me aught, and purify My House for those who make the circuit and stand to pray and bow and prostrate themselves (unto Me).

And proclaim among the people the Pilgrimage: they will come to you on foot and on every lean camel, coming from every remote path."

(Qur'an 22:26-27)

Nearly two million Muslims around the world go in front of Allah together, eliminating any distinction of color, class or race; it demonstrates a marvelous and a unified human effort of submission to One God for a few nights and days. Unity is reflected in diversity.

Muslims go to Mecca, a city initiated by the Mother of Ishmael with her infant son, as Prophet Abraham (p.b.u.t) brought them to this place with the instructions from his Creator.

It does take physical efforts to perform Hajj, but the psychological, spiritual, social, and global gains are tremendous. Muslims believe that after sincerely performing the Hajj, one is transformed and purified as if one has just arrived in this world from a mother's womb.

In response to the call of their Lord issued through Prophet Abraham (p.b.u.h), the pilgrims call:

'Labbaik, Allahumma Labbaik!
'La Sharika lak Labbaik'
'Innal-Hamd laka wan-Ne'mata laka'
'Wal Mulka laka Labbaik'

Translation:

Yes, here I am O' Allah, here I am.
There is no partner for thee. Yes, here I am.
Verily, the Praise and the bounties are Thine.
And the Dominion is Thine. Yes. I am here,
O Allah!

Jihad

Jihad actually means to strive in the way of God. There are various ways, however, that a faithful strives, with the ultimate goal in mind – Submission to God.

The first and foremost, and the greatest Jihad is called *Jihad bin Nafs* - the striving against one's own rebellious self. Improvement of self is the natural outcome of Jihad bin Nafs.

"Go forth light and heavy, and strive hard in Allah's way with your property and your persons; this is better for you, if you know." (Qur'an 9:41)

Striving in the way of God by sacrificing one's wealth is another category of Jihad called *Jihad bil Maal.*

Struggling to spread the knowledge, for the benefit of those, who need it is called *Jihad bil Ilm* – yet another kind of Jihad.

"The Ink of scholars is superior near God than the blood of Martyr"- Prophet Muhammad (S). There should be no intention of worldly gains in this Jihad either.

Since Peace is the goal, and reconciliation is the first alternative in Islam, *Jihad bis Saif* or Jihad by sword is the last resort, used as the line of defense to defend the lives of Muslims and their faith.

"And what reason have you that you should not fight in the way of Allah and for the weak among the men and the women and the children, who (in helplessness) say O our Lord! Take us out of this town whose inhabitants are tyrants and appoint for us from Thee a guardian and appoint for us from Thee a helper." "...And do not exceed the limits, surely Allah does not love those who exceed limits." (Qur'an 4:75; 2:192)

"And if they incline to peace, then incline to it and trust in Allah ..." (Qur'an 8:61)

It is important to realize that not everyone can raise the emblem of Jihad bis Saif in Islam. Fighting for the sake of territorial and monarchial ambitions could be called anything but Submission to God.

“There is no obedience in transgression. You should only obey when you are ordered to do what is good.” prophet Muhammad (S)**

Even this category of Jihad is subject to restrictions, for instance: harming ladies, children, and elderly is prohibited; interference with the monks and hermits who live in monasteries and caves is prohibited; and unnecessarily cutting down trees and destroying fruit bearing trees are prohibited…etc.

In other words, even the defensive practices cannot escape the highly human and moral boundaries, because if they do then the act could be considered anything but the submission to the will of Merciful God.

** From the selection of the Sayings of Prophet Muhammad (S) by Neal Robinson.

There have been a few serious concerns appeared on the horizons of the Muslim community from time to time that slowed down their progress, and in some cases brought them to the verge of desperation when they ignored the warnings. Qur'an has warned its followers to be aware, and not to fall victims to these damaging elements. For example, when people, entered the house of Islam without any intention to acquire peace, they inflicted injuries on its household. An environment slowly emerged, where sincere Muslims, such as Abudhar, who intended nothing but peace, faced miseries and death or were sent into exile. Their objections to injustices were not tolerated. Such environments have often emerged, where peaceful Muslims suffered in their native countries by the hands of those who disguised themselves as Muslims, yet their conducts reflected a direct conflict with Islam. Their sincerity to Islam is questionable.

An in-depth and unbiased observation shows that the image of Islam they tend to create is principally in opposition to Islam.

"And do not incline to those who are unjust," (Qur'an 11:113)

"And (as for) the believing men and the believing women, they are guardians of each other; they enjoin good and forbid evil..." (Qur'an 9:71)

In the same context, the lack of understanding of true leadership has been exploited for ages. It has not only caused distress, but also destroyed the collective efforts of peace, prosperity, and progress that marked the advent of Islam. Many of the so-called leaders, who have been quite often imposed on the Muslims, did not only fail to understand the true essence of Islam, but exploited valuable resources for their own selfishness, and committed injustices against Islam and its followers – their fellow citizens and countrymen.

"And if you obey most of those in the earth, they will lead you astray..." (Qur'an 6:116)

"I swear by time,
Most surely human being is in loss,

Except those who believe and do good, and enjoin on each other truth, and enjoin on each other patience."
(Qur'an 103:1-3)

There are many requirements of true leadership in Islam, and it is the responsibility of the Muslims communities around the globe to make *intelligent* decisions regarding leadership.

"Only Allah is your guardian and His Apostle and those who establish prayers and pay the poor-rate while they bow in prayers."
(Qur'an 5:55)

"...you enjoin what is right and forbid the wrong..."
(Qur'an 3:110)

Muslims are asked to be vigilant as there are historical examples in Qur'an where leadership determined the fate of its followers.

"...Imams who guided by Our command, and We revealed to them the doing of good..." (Qur'an 21:73)

Doing justice individually and socially is actually an important part of Islamic teachings. Doing justice to one's self, keeping one's self in balance, and to make sure that one is physically, psychologically, and spiritually healthy are crucial parts of being a Muslim. This also translates into a functionally healthy and peaceful society. Ignoring these teachings could bring about nothing but lack of peace.

Male or Female

"And (as for) the believing men and the believing women, they are guardians of each other; they enjoin good and forbid evil..." (Qur'an 9:71)

"That I will not waste the work of a worker among you, whether male or female, the one of you being from the other..." (Qur'an 3:195)

"O you human beings! Surely We have created you of a male and a female, and made you tribes and families that you may know each other; surely the most honorable of you with Allah is the one among you most careful (of one's duty)" (Qur'an 49:13)

"Surly the men who submit and the women who submit, and the believing men and the believing women, and the obeying men and the obeying women, and the truthful men and the truthful women, and the patient men and the patient women, and the humble men and the humble women, and the almsgiving men and the almsgiving women, and the fasting men and the fasting women, and the men who guard their private parts and the women who guard, and the men who remember Allah and the women who remember - Allah has prepared for them forgiveness and a mighty reward."

(Qur'an 33:35)

The Resurrection and the Hereafter

There is a sublime wisdom interrelated with justice behind every creation. The universe is the manifestation of this Divine wisdom and justice. Everything is moving to attain perfection, as it is set to attain its goal.

Human beings are also set to attain perfection, but unlike many other creations in this world, they were given a certain level of freedom to shape their own destiny, as they would be accounted for their achievements. Human beings came into existence with an amazing combination of material and spiritual realities. They were given inner selves, souls, and material bodies with the capacity to retain souls. The universal admiration, and support for superior human aspects such as justice, fairness, trustworthiness, and truthfulness represent the awareness of human soul.

"By the soul and Him Who made it perfect, and inspired it to understand what is right and wrong for it;" (Qur'an 91:7-8)

"Allah has made faith beloved to you and adorned it to your hearts, and He has made hateful to you unbelief and transgression and disobedience…" (Qur'an 49:7)

"And certainly We created human being of an extract of clay, then We made him a small seed in a firm resting place, then We made the seed a clot, then We made the clot a lump of flesh, then We made the lump of flash bones, then *We caused it to grow into another creation*, so blessed be Allah, the best of the creators." (Qur'an 23:12-14)

"Then He completed the creation of (human) and breathe into him of His spirit… Little is it that you give thanks." (Qur'an 32:9)

Human beings, with higher capacities, were made responsible to do justice and to act wisely to themselves and to others. They were given the capacity and choice to either attain harmony, and a peaceful destiny or self-destruct a few or all possibilities of attaining perfection. In this lifetime they were also given the capacity to change directions either way.

Attaining perfection by choice is one of the aspects that define human beings, and it is against Divine justice to allow those, who struggled throughout their lives to attain peace and promote justice, to come to an unjust and abrupt end. Yet there are numerous cases recorded by human history, where apparently the lives of the virtuous and the innocents have come to an abrupt and disastrous end.

An in-depth study reveals that human beings were not created for annihilation, and it is actually against the justice that marks the founding principle of this universe to accept any type of injustice. According to Islamic teachings human beings continue their journeys beyond this world towards a particular destiny with much more awareness than they ever had before they close their eyes. On their way, as a Divine decree, they *reap what they sowed* on earth, a process that begins during their lifetime.

From the time of conception to their last breath on this earth, human beings go through amazing transition; from the womb to this world, and from this world to the next. But people with a particular mindset and lack of knowledge and understanding of the incredible realities of life, often fail to see, yet another change.

"Does human being think that We shall not gather his bones? Yea! We are able to make complete even the tips of his fingers"

(Qur'an 75:3-4)

"He is Allah Who began creation and then restores it to its original form after death and dispersal. This restoring is quite easy for Him."

(Qur'an 30:27)

"The day of resurrection is in truth the day on which deeds shall be weighed." (Qur'an 7:8)

"And seek, by means of what Allah has given you, the abode in hereafter…" (Qur'an 28:77)

Jesus son of Mary

"And when the angels said: O Mary! Surely Allah has chosen you and purified you and chosen you above the women of the world.

O Mary! Keep to obedience to your Lord and humble yourself, and bow down with those who bow.

This is of the announcement relating to the unseen which We reveal to you; and you were not with them when they cast their pens (to decide) which of them should have Mary in his charge, and you were not with them when they contended one with another.

When the angel said: O Mary, surely Allah gives you good news with a Word from Him (of one) whose name is the Messiah, Isa (Jesus) son of Mary, worthy of regard in this world and the hereafter and of those who are made near (to Allah).

And he shall speak to the people when in the cradle and when of old age, and (he shall be) one of the good ones.

She said: My Lord! When shall there be a son (born) to me, and man has not touched me? He said: Even so,

Allah creates what He pleases; when He has decreed a matter, He only says to it, Be and it is.

And He will teach him the Book and the wisdom and the Taurat and the Injeel.

And (make him) an apostle to the children of Israel: That I have come to you with a sign from your Lord, that I determine for you out of dust like the form of a bird, then I breath into it and it becomes a bird with Allah's permission and I heal the blind and leprous, and bring the dead to life with Allah's permission and I inform you of what you should eat and what you should store in your houses; most surely there is sign in this for you, if you are believers.

And a verifier of that which is before me of the Taurat, and that I may allow you part of that which has been forbidden unto you, and I have come to you with a sign from your Lord, therefore be careful of (your duty to) Allah and obey me.

Surely Allah is my Lord and your Lord, therefore serve Him; this is the right path.

But when (Isa) Jesus perceived unbelief on their part, he said: Who will be my helpers in Allah's way? The disciples said: We are helpers (in the way) of Allah; We believe in Allah and bear witness that we are submitting ones." (Qur'an 3:42-52)

An Islamic Requirement:

"say: We believe in Allah and that which had been revealed to us, and that which was revealed to Ibrahim (Abraham) and Ismail (Ishmael) and Ishaq (Isaac) and Yaqoub (Jacob) and the tribes, and that which was given to Musa (Moses) and Isa (Jesus), and that which was given to the prophets from their Lord we do not make any distinction between any of them, and to Him do we submit."

(Qur'an 2:136)

A few objective views on Islam

'The creed of Mohamed is free from...ambiguity and the Koran is a glorious testimony to the unity of God.' (Gibbon in his "Decline and Fall of the Roman Empire").

'In a century where scientific truth has dealt a deathblow to religious belief in the Western world, it is precisely the discoveries of science that, in an objective examination of the Islamic revelation, have highlighted the divine character of Qur'an... These scientific considerations should not make us forget that the Qur'an remains a religious book par excellence.' (Dr. Maurice Bucaille – The Qur'an and Modern Science).

'Law which is binding on all from the crowned head to the meanest subject, is a law interwoven with a system of the wisest, the most learned and the most enlightened jurisprudence that ever existed in the world.' (English statesman and orator Edmund Burke

on Islamic Law in his “Impeachment of Warren Hastings”).

‘The more I study the more I discover that the strength of Islam does not lie in the sword.’ (Mahatma Gandhi in “Young India”).

‘As I read Qur’an, I find those dynamic principles of life, not mystic but practical ethics for the daily conduct of life suited to the whole world.’ (The Indian scholar and famous poetess of India, Sarojini Naidu, in a lecture on the Ideals of Islam – Madras, India, 1918).

The Food

Being a Muslim is an individual as well as social responsibility. A true Muslim is recognized by his/hers deeds rather than words. Among other things a Muslim is responsible for doing justice. One is supposed to be just to oneself, to fellow human beings (*Muslims or non-Muslims*), to the surroundings one lives in, and even to the animals. Thus the Islamic out look is sacred, yet practical and peaceful.

Keeping oneself clean, and physically, psychologically, and spiritually healthy is an elementary but a crucial responsibility prescribed by Islam. This would not only include pursuing a healthy lifestyle, but abstaining from anything that may be harmful in either short term or in long run. Therefore, consuming alcohol, and some meat (e.g., pork), or other edible animal products that are not prepared as per Islamic statute, are among the few items prohibited in Islam. The underlying factor behind these abstinences is the human and social health.

*Some of the words**
of
Prophet Muhammad (S)

*A few of the spoken words recorded in the following pages reflect only some aspects and actual character of the teachings that quench the thirst of a Muslim spirit. These *Hadiths (Words spoken by the Prophet (S)) mentioned in this section are part of Islamic teachings alongside Qur'an the revealed book.*

“Verily, deeds depend upon the intentions.”

(Source: Muttafaqunalayih)

"Luqman al-Hakim made his will and counseled his son, saying, my son! Sit with the learned men and keep close to them. Allah gives life to the hearts with the light of wisdom as Allah gives life to the dead earth with the abundant rain of the sky."

(Source: Malik's Muwatta)

"You have come to ask about righteousness?" … "Consult your heart. Righteousness is that about which the soul feels tranquil and the heart feels tranquil, and wrongdoing is that which wavers in the soul and moves to and from in the breast even though people again and again have given you their legal opinion (in its favor)."

(Sources: Musnads of Ahmed bin Hanbal & Al-Darimi)

"Plenty of provision or abundance do not make a person rich and wealthy; real richness is the benevolence of heart."

(Sources: Muslim and Bukhari)

"The great Jihad is that for the conquest of self."

(Source: Bukhari)

“The best of you are those who have the best morals.”

(Source: Bukhari)

“Kindness is a mark of faith, and whoever is not kind has no faith.”

(Source: Muslim)

"Each person's every joint must perform a charity every day the sun comes up: to act justly between two people is a charity; to help a man with his mount, lifting him onto it or hoisting up his belongings onto it is a charity; a good word is a charity, every step you take to prayers is a charity and removing a harmful thing from the road is a charity."

(Sources: Muslim and Bukhari)

"The best of charity is that, which the right hand gives and the left hand knows not of."

(Source: Bukhari)

“The believer is not the one who eats his fill when the neighbor beside him is hungry.”

(source: Baihaqi)

"None of you (truly) believes until he wishes for his brother what he wishes for himself."

(Sources: Muslim and Bukhari)

"The most excellent jihad is when one speaks a true word in the presence of a tyrannical ruler."

(Source: Tirmidhi)

"Avoid cruelty and injustice…and guard yourselves against miserliness, for this has ruined nations who lived before you."

(Source: Riyadh-us-Salaheen)

“A mischief maker will not enter paradise.”

(Sources: Muslim and Bukhari)

"He who is not trustworthy has no Faith, and he who does not keep his Covenant has no religion."

(Source: Baihaqi)

“Fasting is a shield and a powerful fortress.”

(Sources: Ahmad & Baihaqi)

“Whichever habit a believer may acquire he does not acquire the habit of falsehood and treachery.”

(Source: Islam a code of social life)

"Help your brother, whether he is an oppressor or he is an oppressed one." People asked, "O Allah's Apostle! It is all right to help him if he is oppressed, but how should we help him if he is an oppressor?" The Prophet said, "By preventing him from oppressing others."

(Source: Bukhari)

"An hour of justice is better than a year of prayer."

(Source: Nahjul-Fasaha)

"There are four signs of a sincere person,
1) his heart is sound
2) his limbs are harmless
3) he does good to others
4) he refrains from doing evil."

(Source: Islam a code of social life)

"The one who will be dearest to God and nearest to Him in the station on the Day of Resurrection will be a just imam and the one who will be most hateful to God on the Day of Resurrection, and will receive the severest punishment will be a tyrannical imam"

(Source: Tirmidhi)

"Who ever of you observes an evil (in society) must change it (object over it) physically with his hand, so if he does not have the power of it then he must object over it by his tongue, and if he does not have the strength of that, he must object upon it in his heart (he must not remain indifferent to it). And this is the lowest status of faith."

(Source: Musnad Ahmed ibn Hanbal)

"One who comes to a rich man and show humbleness to him for the sake of his wealth has lost two third of his religion."

(Source: Tuhful Aqool)

"There are only two types of persons you should envy: the man to whom God has given wealth and the power to spend it all in the cause of truth, and the one to whom God has given wisdom and who judges by it and teaches it."

(Source: Bukahari)

"The treasures of knowledge are opened by asking questions. May Allah bless you. Ask questions because four persons are rewarded: the questioner, the speaker, the hearer and their friends."

(Source: Islam a code of social life)

“Seeking knowledge is a duty of every Muslim male and female”

(Sources: Tirmidhi and Muslim)

“The person who goes in search of knowledge is on active service for God until he returns.”

(Sources: Mishkat al-Masabih & Tirmidhi)

"It is better to sit alone than in company with the bad; and it is better still to sit with the good than alone. It is better to speak to a seeker of knowledge than to remain silent; but silence is better than idle words."

(Source: Bukhari)

"Allah will not be merciful to those who are not merciful to mankind."

(Source: Bukhari)

"The best among you is he who cooperates with his family."

(Source: Jamiasa'adat)

"Observe justice in dealing with your children in the same manner in which you expect them to observe justice in being kind and good to you."

(Source: Makarmul Akhlaq)

"Allah blesses those, who assist their children in doing good things which they do themselves."

(Source: Islam dar qalb-e-Ijtima)

“Feed the Hungry, visit the sick and set captives free.”

(Source: Bukhari)

"One Muslim should do six acts of kindness to another: he should salute him when he meets him, accept his invitation when he gives one, say 'Allah have mercy on you' when he sneezes, visit him when he is ill, follow his bier when he dies, and like for him what he likes for himself."

(Sources: Tirmidhi & Darimi)

"The true Muslim is one whose tongue and hand other Muslims do not fear"

(Source: Bukhari)

Holy Prophet (S) once asked: "Who is that person among you who loves the property of his successor more than his own property? The Companions submitted: 'O Messenger of God (S) there is none among us who loves his successor's property more than his own.' He said: Then his property is which he has sent ahead; and that which he retains belongs to his successor."

(Source: Bukhari)

"By God! What is this world compared with the Hereafter! It is like dipping your finger in the sea, look how little remains on it when you withdraw it."

(Source: Mishkat al-Masabih)

"Kindness to any living creature will be rewarded."

(Source: Bukhari)

Note: Hadith number 24, 27, 33, 35, and 38 in the previous section were taken from the book *Sayings of Muhammad* (S) by Neal Robinson – Published by Ecco Press in 1991.

Please send

comments or questions regarding the book

or the topics covered in the book to:

questbypen@yahoo.com

About the Author

The author has taught undergraduate courses covering Global History, World Religions, and International Relations. His published articles discuss World Politics, Education, and various topics in Science and Technology - as he further specializes in Computer Logic and Electronics.

www.ingramcontent.com/pod-product-compliance
Ingram Content Group UK Ltd.
Pitfield, Milton Keynes, MK11 3LW, UK
UKHW041821200726
13854UKWH00001BA/262

9 781410 707796